THE WAR YEARS
by "One Small Wren"

THE WAR YEARS
by "One Small Wren"

Lilian Pickering

ATHENA PRESS
LONDON

THE WAR YEARS by "One Small Wren"
Copyright © Lilian Pickering 2006

ISBN 1 84401 658 7

First Published 2006 by
ATHENA PRESS
Queen's House, 2 Holly Road
Twickenham TW1 4EG
United Kingdom

Printed for Athena Press

To all my friends, Canadian and English, in the Vancouver WRCNS Association.

Also to Sarah, without whose keen interest this book would never have been typed.

What inspired me to join up? I think that my early life had conditioned me for it. A war baby, I was just two years old when World War One ended, but old enough to know that everything, even my toys and books, had been altered by that great event that had happened – The War.

"Prices were never as high as this before The War," said the grown-ups, or – "This was never done before The War." And if I fell and banged my knees, I would be exhorted not to cry, but "be brave, like the soldiers."

Aunt Nancy was my father's sister, and a very gifted teacher; she taught grammar school boys during the war. She could interest any child and make him or her want to know more – even Latin or maths! History was her great interest, and we used to work out Nelson's famous battles on the nursery floor. She would be down there with us, making maps with coloured marbles, and reenacting the big battles with a fleet of little empty china pans that had held watercolour paints.

From Aunt Nancy, I understood that our fighting men had to do many difficult and disagreeable things in order to keep us all safe, and that *nothing* that we could do for them in return was too good for them.

It was only after I had grown up that I learnt that her best friend's brother, who undoubtedly would have married her, had been killed in that war.

In later years, Aunt Nancy told me how her friend, Olive, had brought Alan's regimental buttons and emblems to her and said, "He would have wished you to have them."

"And I had never even *thought* of such a thing," Aunt Nancy recalled. Nevertheless, the buttons and other items were carefully wrapped and were still among her things when she died, aged eighty-nine.

Later on at school, the girls would talk about war and peace. I think, subconsciously, we all knew that another war would come; the girls thought that "next time" we would be fighting against the French, and not the Germans – it turned out to be half true.

As the threat of war started to emerge and the Women's Services were reconstituted in 1937, I would have liked to volunteer; as I was a Sea

Ranger with my Signaller's Badge, it seemed natural to choose the Wrens – however, it seemed unlikely to happen, as my father, a doctor running a small private sanatorium for TB, had me as his secretary, living at home – a "reserved occupation", which meant that I could not be called up, although I longed to "do my bit".

However, by 1941, that problem was solved by a patient, a young businessman, who was now fit to work under medical supervision, but could not live in his home, war-torn Manchester.

We were used to seeing the northern sky every night, red with the reflection of the flames from Manchester and Liverpool. As we lived out in the country, we soon learnt to distinguish between the engines of British and German planes on their way to these cities; we would fall asleep with both overhead and hoped – or prayed – that the British would be faster. "Oh, well, either way, they'll hit us or they won't!" – and we would carefully hide all our lights every night.

The blackout, though the subject of many stage jokes, was no joke in reality, but a thorough nuisance! We had to keep the various black curtains blocking out every tiniest beam of light, with patients who had to have open windows and plenty of fresh air! This took much time and work – but it had to be done, as the smallest light, even a lit cigarette, might be seen by the Germans on their way home (perhaps with unused bombs on-board) – or we could be reported by the RAF, who would report us if any light showed. A farmhouse a mile or so away was hit and demolished. We felt the "thump" through to our side of the mountain. Local talk said that no one was in the farmhouse except an old woman (who was killed), and she must have inadvertently shown a streak of light for a moment, right under an enemy plane – no one in their senses would have shown a lit window!

The foregoing patient, then, accepted the offer of my job and took my place in the office. With some trepidation, I then applied to "join the Wrens and free a man to join the Fleet", as the advertisements said.

First, I had to travel to Chester for an interview with a rather discouraging Chief Wren, who seemed to think that there were no vacancies in any category that I wanted – particularly in wireless telegraphy (W/T), which I fancied, as I knew the Morse Code. After enquiring about one or two other categories, I finally told her that I would do *anything*, or go *anywhere*, if *only* I could get into the Wrens! There, the interview ended. Soon afterwards, I was called up for training in Dundee, Scotland – as a W/T operator!

But before my call-up notice could take effect, there was the *Altmark*. The *Altmark* was a German prison ship, operating in northern waters, carrying the captains of a number of merchant ships that had been captured by the Germans and their officers transferred to the hold of the prison ship – a totally illegal action, as merchant shipping was supposed to be neutral and without hindrance in wartime.

Up until this point, I had belonged to a Voluntary Aid Detachment (VAD) in a nearby town, and it was known that the husband of one of our members was a prisoner on the *Altmark*; our whole detachment was anxiously waiting for news of that ship, as was all England. Every BBC bulletin seemed to carry news of naval ships that had "just missed" the *Altmark*; she appeared to have a genius for slipping unhindered through the northern waters or otherwise evading capture – she was believed to be making for a Norwegian port. No one knew if the prisoners were alive or dead – had their captors shot them? or worse?

Some days after my call-up notice was received, we heard on the six o'clock radio news that the *Altmark* had been found – making eastward, as was supposed – by *HMS Cossack*, a ship we had not previously heard of. *Cossack* had stopped the German ship, sending a boarding party to seize and search her. All the same, *Altmark*'s captain had denied that he carried any prisoners, which was nonsense – we all *knew* they were there!

The ship was searched – without success! This

was impossible! One deck hatch remained un-opened, and the searchers were assured that only bilge water was below. Nevertheless, the boat-swain in charge of the search party ordered the hatch to be opened. With our whole family gath-ered around the wireless set in our drawing room – like hundreds of others in Britain – we heard the challenge from the prisoners in the dark below, who appeared to have lost none of their spirits! (They had heard the noise overhead without knowing what was happening); and then the reply came, "The Navy's here!" (I nearly hit the ceiling with pride upon hearing this!) Then the boat-swain's next question was answered: "We're *all* here!" (– according to the BBC reporter on board, who named the speaker – our member's hus-band!). I would guess that the phone lines in Colwyn Bay, eight miles away, were jammed with calls to our member's number to pass on the good news! The prisoners were brought from below, and the names of Captain Vian and the *Cossack* were hailed throughout Britain – which had badly needed a victory in the West at that time.

In due time, I set off for Dundee but, arriving in Manchester, a porter rushed me and my luggage on to the wrong train, just as it was leaving Man-chester – and so I did not arrive in Dundee until two o'clock the next morning. It took quite a while to dawn on me that this confusion may have been due to overnight bombing in Manchester. Be that as it may, I was peeved to find myself in Leeds (Yorkshire) at about one o'clock, with no train to York before ten o'clock that night – when I had expected to be there by two! However, nothing daunted, after finding some lunch, I also found a bus to take me to nearby Gomersal, to visit my two aunts and uncles who lived there, and any cousins who might be at home. My appearance was a total surprise, and I was welcomed to a real and complete "Yorkshire Tea" – everything one could think of as though that was the last meal I would ever eat! – before the family saw me to the bus back to Leeds, to catch the York train at ten o'clock.

We arrived at Dundee at two o'clock the following morning on a crowded train, with all the compartments full and passengers sitting on their luggage in the corridors. The station names were all blocked out (to hinder any possible parachutists) and I almost missed getting off the train! I was saved by two Highland soldiers, who wouldn't let the train leave till I had collected my luggage from my compartment.

A porter was waiting and I said, "I want a taxi, to take me to Mathers Hotel."

"Ye'll no' be wantin' a taxi tae go tae Mathers," he said. (Shades of my early childhood on hearing that speech! I had come home!) He set off for the station entrance while I followed, wondering. Outside the station was a square, of which the whole opposite side was taken up by a large building. Across the front was a huge notice: "MATHERS HOTEL".

"Yon's Mathers," the porter said. "Go straight on. Ye'll no' be wantin' a taxi," and he took my two cases across the square and dumped them on the doorstep. These were the Wrens' quarters – and most of the inhabitants were sleeping.

In the cold, dark dawn, I stood on the steps of the hotel and rang the bell, wondering if anyone would be up, and would I be reprimanded for arriving a day late? Fortunately, my fears were groundless; the firewatchers and household staff were on duty and I was able to sit and drink a mug of cocoa with those firewatchers who were not on the roof (and they informed me about various matters concerning the course) until everyone was awake and I could be taken to my cabin for some sleep.

I learned that our group would be the Second Division, the First Division having already been there for six weeks. The ship's complement would be made up when the Third Division came, in another six weeks. The divisions were called after warships; the First Division had taken the name of "Rodney", a battleship. When our turn came after six weeks, we chose "Cossack", which was still in the news; it spoke of action and smartness, and sounded "snappy" in drill commands! The Third Division, when it came, took the name of "Renown"; and the household staff were "Furious"; as a few of them disliked this and took it as a personal description, I used to picture them as "furiously wielding brooms and dusters"!

The training was a two-year course, taken at Dundee Wireless College – but we had to cover the work in six months, plus the relevant naval signalling procedures. We were marched daily in our divisions to and from college. Dundee had trams which ran, ting-tinging, at the elbows of the outer file. If anyone drew back, our divisional officer would call out, "*Swing* those arms there!" – and we would defy the trams to take "those arms" off at the elbows.

The course included long periods of taking down Morse; learning how to transmit; and practising the naval way of signalling. We were divided into classes of twenty or so within our divisions. Our class instructor was a young man – probably in his early twenties – at first very abashed at finding himself in charge of a class of women, mostly considerably older than himself. But, "There's a war on!" – we ragged him cheerfully, and he got used to us, and learned to call us by our surnames.

A group of four (who later featured large in the

Christmas pantomime) would sometimes enter-
tain us with a quartet, before classes could begin.
Favourites were "Don't Fence Me In" or "Ragtime
Cowboy Joe". Occasionally I hear these songs on
the wireless; they never fail to bring up the vision
of these four performing at the start of class. Our
spirits were high, we remained good friends and
we were all quite sad at parting at the end of the
course!

We also had to practice naval signalling procedure. The RN telegraphist who taught us this had
served in the Mediterranean under Lord Louis
Mountbatten, who, according to him, was a
stickler for correct procedure. Between sessions of
practising, he told us stories of W/T under "Lord
Louis" – "when you're sitting on a wave in the
Mediterranean". A few people found the long
hours of concentrating on Morse too much for
them and were transferred to other training – but
most of us survived.

We went through the preliminary WRNS
training in our "spare" time, and in two weeks
were "signed on" and got our uniforms. All the
buttons on our greatcoats and uniform jackets
were ordinary black buttons, and we were told we
must buy the crested black uniform buttons at a
naval tailor's shop – of which there were many in
Dundee. Another new recruit and I went shopping
together, for buttons of various sizes. On entering

one such shop and looking at the buttons, she remarked, "I like the brass ones that some of them are wearing – I think I'll have those." I was properly scandalised! Even I knew that all above petty officers wore brass buttons, as I had learned at Sea Rangers. "You can't wear *those* – they're for officers!" I cried very hastily – fortunately she believed me, and changed to black.

Christmas came in the middle of our course, and with it, a week's leave – and an outbreak of mumps! I woke up with the latter on the morning we were to go on leave. My cabin mates, keeping well away from me, escorted me to the entrance to sickbay, before we got dressed – "Don't *come near* us!" – and there I spent a fairly easy-going Christmas, as regards naval discipline. Then I was sent on leave, to wait until my quarantine was over – and finally returned, to make up for time lost on the course.

The exams taken and passed, we were sent our separate ways, with many promises to write to friends; with three others I was sent to Greenock, on the Clyde. We were quartered in the Western Hotel, a small Wrenery near the river, with about twenty or so Wrens in the charge of a quarters petty officer and her helpers.

Most other Wrens living there were M/T drivers (driving the officers in their cars), or dispatch riders (carrying dispatches on their motorcycles).

A much larger Wrenery (Mariners) was being prepared further up the hillside for the many Wrens expected. The W/T office, to which we reported after our arrival, was only about ten minutes' walk away, and was one of a series of huts in the grounds of a large house, which was the admiral's headquarters.

We were a branch of Western Approaches – quite an important station, as a number of the convoys from Canada came into the Clyde and we W/T Wrens also had to look after the coastal W/T traffic. We worked four watches, so there was one Wren on each watch, along with a sailor, or maybe two (who gradually disappeared to sea) – all in the charge of a PO tel, who though friendly, was fair and expected high standards of work. We were shown all that went on; but it was a fearful moment when one of the sailors stood up, put his headphones on me, and sat me down in front of the set. Fortunately, all we saw coincided with what we had learned on our course in Dundee – and when someone thrust an R/T (spoken) message for a local trawler into my hand, I was able to read it off into the microphone. The ship answered immediately (rather to the dismay of the men, as they said they had been calling her for two days) on hearing the voice of the first Wren in that section of Western Approaches!

However, that did not alter the necessity on our

part for extreme vigilance over all ships out at sea. We had never, on watch on the port wave, to be found with our headphones off – "not even if the Admiral or your top Wren Officer comes in," as the PO said, "you carry on and take no notice." However, we all got into the way of things, and I thoroughly enjoyed the work. There was also an area broadcast, which had to be read and "passed through" to the SDO as necessary.

When I was on summer leave, a draft came through for me to go to Petersfield in Hampshire, to be trained as a petty officer instructor, teaching W/T recruits at the new communications training establishment, which had been moved from Dundee to Warrington – just an hour by train from home. Unfortunately, instead of recalling me from leave, the leading telegraphist then in charge of the office, chose to send another Wren instead of me, and so I missed my chance of promotion. I then volunteered for overseas service.

Early in December, I was given my Christmas leave and was able to join my family in London, where they were spending a week. Miraculously, there was no blitz during the time we were there, though there was, of course, much devastation. One morning we stood on a rise, looking east across London; at a distance was a half-demolished building, which was the main Post Office. As we watched, a long line of little figures in blue uniform appeared, clambering out of the building and over the rubble – all with large sacks slung over their shoulders. On inquiry, we were told that these were the London postmen, carrying out (as they did every day) their task of seeing that the mail got through.

Back at Greenock, I was "sitting on" the broadcast one afternoon; all was quiet – when suddenly pandemonium broke loose on the air! The broadcast started at high speed, one long priority message after another; the landline began clacking rapidly, and a sailor came over to help me, tearing the messages off the pads and sending them through to the SDO as quickly as he could. (I hated that landline at the best of times; one had to read the long and short spaces between the clicks, which I always found difficult.) There were instructions to rebroadcast some of the very long messages (over 200 groups in some cases) on other frequencies – no time to fill in the delivery instructions or sort out the messages – my helper took all that over – and still the messages piled up.

Day after day this would occur, and on the afternoon watch, one could count on writing nonstop at high speed until the watch finished at 8 p.m. Of course we all knew that "something big" was on, but we might never know what it was – more of this later.

At Greenock I experienced my first Christmas,

With a South African WAAF friend in Cape Town

Out shopping in Cape Town

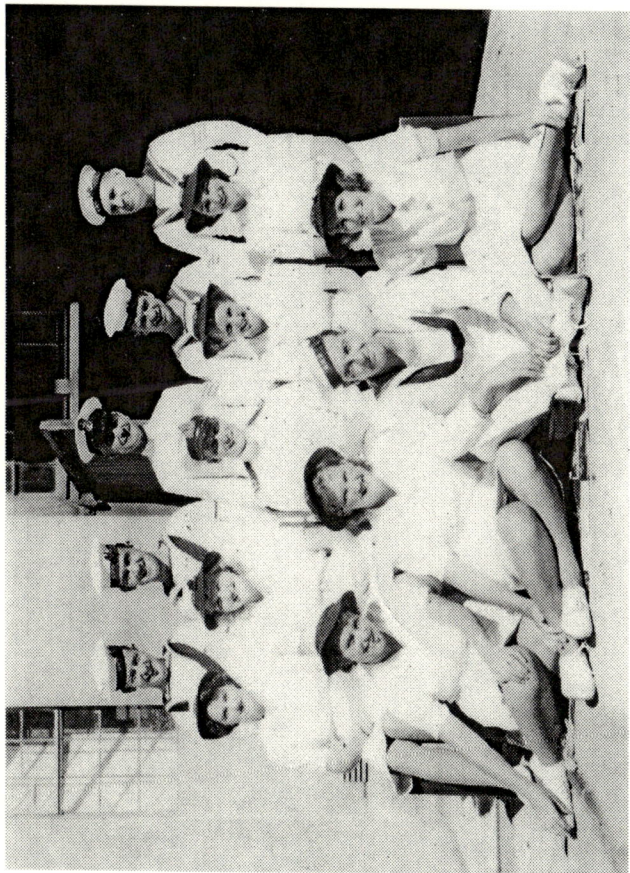

Command Headquarters W/T staff, Cape Town

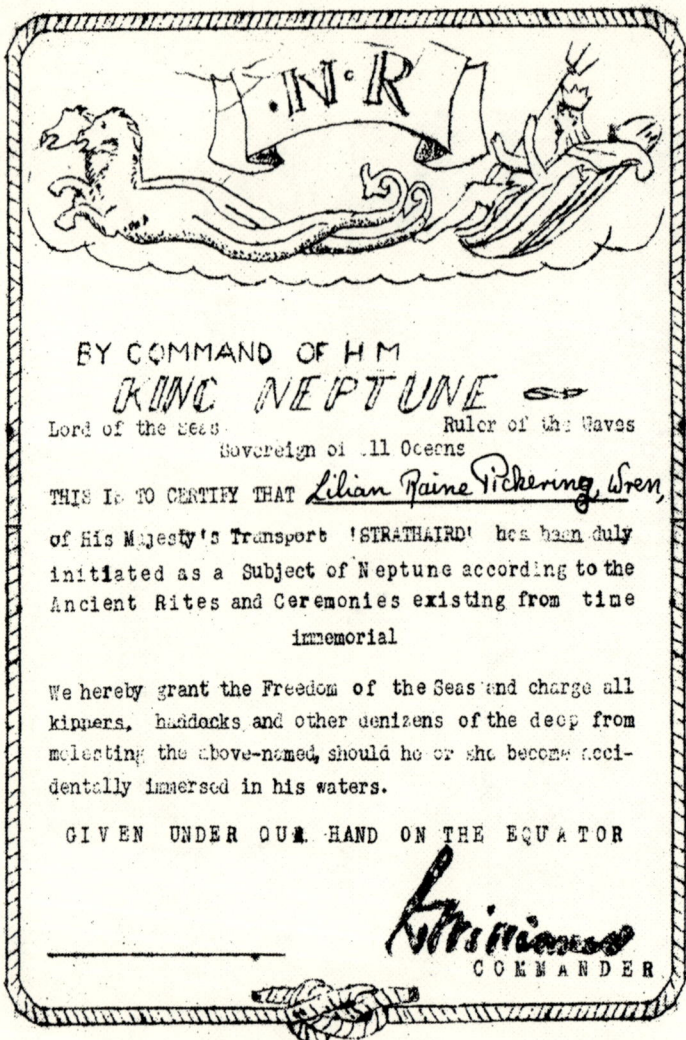

BY COMMAND OF H M

KING NEPTUNE

Lord of the Seas   Ruler of the Waves
Sovereign of all Oceans

THIS IS TO CERTIFY THAT *Lilian Raine Pickering, Wren,*

of His Majesty's Transport 'STRATHAIRD' has been duly

initiated as a Subject of Neptune according to the

Ancient Rites and Ceremonies existing from time

immemorial

We hereby grant the Freedom of the Seas and charge all

kippers, haddocks and other denizens of the deep from

molesting the above-named, should he or she become acci-

dentally immersed in his waters.

GIVEN   UNDER   OUR   HAND   ON THE   EQUATOR

COMMANDER

Certificate received for crossing the equator (see p.25)

(see p.25)

Navy-style. In January I said farewell to Greenock, and went home on embarkation leave, followed by three weeks at the overseas depot in Golden Square, London. I had been told to take a spare suitcase, as we would be issued with tropical kit. I was also told not to tell anyone. My mother, however, told all her friends that she was quite sure that I would be going to Murmansk (a place I had hardly even heard of!) and would be issued with furs. I just smiled and said nothing!

In London, we were under strict secrecy; no one must know that we were to go abroad! "Careless talk costs lives," as the posters said everywhere – and those with anybody in war work, or the three Services, took notice and were careful of imparting to *anyone* *any* details that they came to know.

We were kitted up with white tropical uniform (but kept our blue serge for seasonal changes) and every item had to be marked with our name – for which we were given an afternoon. Much to our chagrin, we had to wear our bluettes (overalls) on board ship, as we could not launder the white uniforms. We were then despatched into London to buy a list of things that we would need – such as white underwear, salt water soap and other items usually associated with summer holidays! "Very suitable for travelling abroad," as one shop assistant said. I tried to look inscrutable! As regards the salt water soap, most ships supplied fresh water for drinking only; salt water soap was said to lather in salt water, which toilet soap would not; though I cannot say I ever noticed much difference! We had lectures on health and hygiene, Navy life overseas, censorship, security – and of course, lots of squad drill!

We left at 10 p.m. one winter evening, creeping out in silence and boarding buses in the dark. We had all written letters home, which the staff would post in three weeks' time, to say that we would now be at sea – but we would not know where we were going until we were actually at sea.

One Wren dropped her tin hat, amid sounds of "Ssh, ssh!" It echoed queerly on the pavement but no one stirred in the street. We were driven to a railway station – King's Cross, some people thought – where we boarded a special train. Then, along came an Army contingent, marching smartly on to the platform, with their sun helmets hanging from the ends of their rifles by the chinstraps for all to see – so much for security!

When our train set off, we were able to get some sleep. In the morning, the petty officers issued us with packed breakfasts on the train until we arrived in Greenock – which I had just left! We were lined up all morning on the quay, standing at ease, and 200 hungry Wrens boarded the ship at 2:10 p.m. Our first question was, "What about lunch?" only to be told, "It's over – there will be a cup of tea and a piece of cake at four o'clock!" It appeared that the delay was caused by 100 Wrens from the previous draft, who had been quarantined for measles and were now on board. The OC troops was protesting against having to take on a further 200 – "his" sergeant majors would have to give up their cabins for us, and let us share their mess – oh dear! (At a later date, the WRNS officer who was censoring our letters would tell us, amid gales of laughter from us, "You *must* make your letters appear as if you are on an ordinary voyage – you *must not mention* the OC troops!") However, we all settled down in the end, and the Wrens and sergeant majors got on quite well.

Next morning when we woke up, we were out in the Atlantic, in a storm, on a P&O liner, with a large convoy all around us and several destroyers protecting us. Our liner was the P&O *Strathaird*, and our sleeping quarters were groups of several cabins with the partitions removed to make one large cabin, with nine double bunks and two mattresses on the deck (twenty Wrens in all), in the care of Harry, the P&O steward, who guided us in matters of life aboard ship. We were just above the waterline – which the several thousand troops on board were not – and we pitied them, and thought we were lucky.

We were given forty-eight hours to get over

seasickness, then a boat drill was held – by order of the OC troops, everyone had to be on deck – "even if they have to hang over the side" – which one or two did. Life jackets were issued to all, without which we were never to be found, and we were informed as to what we should do in an emergency. The fresh air and sea breezes soon revived everyone, and we zigzagged along, watching the sun change from one side of the ship to the other, as the convoy turned. We were told we went nearly to America before turning south.

For two days, far out to sea, we crossed the opening of the Bay of Biscay, home of German submarines, and had to sleep in our clothes for three nights. It was my bath night (with salt water soap!). The bathroom was below the waterline, and as I hastily bathed in semi-darkness, I fervently hoped that any submarine that might be outside would wait until I was out of the bath and into my clothes before pouncing on us – but the convoy sailed safely on with its destroyer escort, and in the morning we were off Gibraltar. One of our destroyers had gone back and sunk a submarine which had tried to escape through the Straits. Years later, I saw that submarine, in the Imperial War Museum in London, marked on a map of submarines sunk. Every ship in the convoy was aware that a "sub" had been dealt with, and each one had people on deck to cheer the destroyer as she rejoined the convoy.

The voyage took six weeks, and we learned that we were going to Durban, South Africa. One evening before dark, a "tombola" – a new name to me – was held – my first introduction to "legs eleven" and "clicketty click" etc. The deck was covered from end to end with people sitting cross-legged, while the men with the loudest voices stood in the doorways of the deck structure and called out the numbers. I don't remember if I won any money – probably not! The ship had to be blacked out around 6 p.m., so we got to bed quite early.

As we got further south, we saw flying fish all around the ship and the weather became warmer. We stopped in at Freetown, Sierra Leone, for two days – but only the officers and a contingent of nurses from another ship were invited to a party ashore. The rest of us – including the troops (overseen by the sergeant majors) – were allowed a bucket of fresh water each to do some laundry.

When we sailed again, we crossed the equator. In these days of flying, that is no big deal – but then, there were initiation ceremonies involving King Neptune, his court, ducking the first-timers in the swimming bath and other high jinks. However, the baths were dry and no high jinks could be held because of the blackout – but we were all given certificates from "King Neptune's Court" to say that we had duly "crossed the line" and been initiated.

Then, one morning, sailing further south, Table Mountain rose out of the mist before us, and we knew we were at Cape Town. The convoy divided in two and the other half sailed into Table Bay, accompanied by two of the destroyers; circling our ship with loud speakers, they played a goodbye. I remember, they played "O, the Pity of it All". Our half of the convoy continued down, around Cape Point, and up the coast towards Durban – another three days, passing the Twelve Apostles Mountains, with high cliffs and pleasant-looking seaside resorts at their foot, forming the backbone of the Cape of Good Hope. Then we sailed past the Southern coast to Durban, where all the people on the docks and up on the bluff were cheering us, as the convoy sailed up the harbour in fine style. The pipes and drums of the 51st Highland Brigade (so we were informed) were on our ship, and they came on deck and played us triumphantly up the harbour among the cheering crowds – it was an occasion to remember! I am afraid that the "welcome singing" by Mrs Perla Sidli was drowned out – I hope she forgave our seeming bad manners, but we simply didn't know she was there until some time later.

In the evening we had shore leave – a river of khaki, white and blue, flowing up to the dock gates and out into Durban, where every car that had any petrol left was waiting to show us around (to say nothing of the rickshaws!). Two RAF men, on leave from West Africa, invited us to share their rickshaw, a coffee and a trip around the sights of Durban before we returned to the ship, after a friendly evening.

The next day, forty of us were disembarked, wearing our whites for the first time. They did look a little bit grey, having been packed for so long – but that was soon remedied when they were laundered. The rest of the draft eventually sailed on further, and we heard, landed at Kilindini, the port for Mombasa. We were sent to work for a week in various offices around Durban. I was sent to the Fleet Mail Office and was put to emptying a bag of mail which had been left unopened. (They were very short-staffed, like many places in those days.) The mail seemed to be following the ships around, as letter after letter would turn up for the same people, bearing many old forwarding addresses; they had always just sailed. One could imagine the recipients wondering why they received no mail.

Even when my bag was finally emptied and sorted, the most prominent recipients had just sailed from Durban. I found it rather sad, but it seemed it couldn't be helped then.

I was able to pay a much-anticipated visit to my South African cousins, some of whom had visited England. My aunt had only to write to my mother, and mention that "Lilian had been to tea", for those at home to know that I had arrived in South Africa.

My aunt's practice was to bake a big fruit cake in a large Sharpe's toffee tin, then put the lid on when it had cooled; seal it with Sellotape and send it home to England – where currants and nuts were rarely seen. Many people just sent food parcels home, but we soon found that they were apt to arrive minus the sugar, so we stopped sending sugar, although it grew there and was plentiful.

My cousins were not very surprised to see me – they had thought I would turn up sooner or later! We were billeted on the lovely, long seafront, in a Durban hotel, and after a week or so we were put on a ship called the *Almanzora*, each with a cabin to herself, returning unescorted to England. (She could sail faster unescorted.) Three days later, we were put ashore in Cape Town, to be met by our First Officer – forty Wrens and their officers, arrived at last! Another fifty Wrens and their officers were there ahead of us – they had been there for six months. We occupied a large hotel, built round a courtyard – the Helmsley – with the annexe across the road.

We had been sent out for the purpose of opening up a base in Cape Town for all the convoys that were expected to be sent east around the

Cape; owing to the fighting around Malta, they could not safely be sent through the Mediterranean. However, we had not been there very long before the siege of Malta (George Cross Island) was raised, and the Mediterranean was safe for ships. Later, the landings were made in Sicily and then Italy; so the convoys seldom came to Cape Town, and we were really not very busy, but had to remain there in case fortunes changed.

During the next four months, six of us were sent daily to work at an air station outside Cape Town, to learn to deal with the only comparable threat – which never materialised – Japanese submarines. All the seaward lights had to be blacked out, otherwise lighting was normal. A loudspeaker van would be sent to offending houses, to park outside and broadcast: "Number so-and-so, you are showing a seaward light in an upstairs window – will you kindly put it out" – or something similar. This would be repeated over and over again – sometimes varied to: "Number so-and-so, you are *still* showing that light – please put it out!" until the light was extinguished, when the van would leave.

However, I found aircraft work totally different from my previous posting in England. Along with several other Wrens, I had been hoping for a draft to Slangkop Radio, the naval and Post Office wireless station about twenty to thirty miles out of

Cape Town. However, a mild struggle was now taking place as to the ability of Wrens to do W/T work (!). This had sometimes happened in Britain, where a number of naval officers had not believed that Wrens could do some of the jobs they had been trained for and did not want them on their stations until they *had* to accept them – and saw what they could do! Finally, at the end of the War, most did not want to part with them. So, we all enjoyed a quiet chuckle at the delay.

Nevertheless, I imagine that our senior officer (backed by us) gently persisted, and finally, after six months, twenty of us, teleprinter operators and "sparkers", were sent out to Slangkop under a petty officer Wren (teleprinter operator).

Slangkop was a Post Office radio station, which had been taken over and expanded by the Royal Navy. There were several Post Office operators, with a senior (civilian) Post Office official in charge, and all of us Navy personnel were under a Chief Petty Officer, Royal Navy.

The sailors (who were nearly all survivors from the *Prince of Wales* and the *Repulse*) lived in a hutted camp at the station, and we were billeted a few miles away in the Kommetje Hotel. We ate in the hotel dining room, but the annexe across the road was generally considered our domain; in it was an unused sitting room, which we used as our "Fo'c'sle". Our bedrooms (one each!) were all in a row on the first floor "stoep" (veranda), and we were treated as civilian guests, with an early morning cup of coffee, which did not always suit watchkeeping times, and some people asked to be excluded and forego the luxury. Certainly, coming off watch at 2 a.m. and having to be on duty again at 8 a.m., it did not seem worthwhile to wake up earlier for coffee! Later, when the hotel changed hands, quarters were built for us on the station; a hut was fenced around and fitted with built-in beds and wood furniture – very nice and comfortable – and half the men's mess was allotted to us, as they had gone to England.

The city of Durban had issued a booklet to the British Forces in South Africa, containing all sorts of information and advice on how to conduct oneself in this strange land, both socially and politically. It was called "Complex Country" – and so it was! So it will hardly surprise anybody to know that the hotel proprietor and his wife were *German*! However, everyone at the W/T station up the road seemed to be on friendly terms with them, and we were well treated, so no harm ever seemed to come of it. On a Saturday night the sailors would occasionally tease Max about having a wireless set hidden in his chimney! He and his wife worked very hard.

We had Navy transport to take us on and off duty, especially at night, but in fine weather we often preferred to walk. Both sides of the road were lined with beautiful flowering gum trees with red, yellow and orange blossoms in the season, giving off their aromatic scent; I have rarely, if ever, seen these anywhere else. There were lots of crayfish in the sea, and we were largely fed on crayfish – crayfish salad, crayfish "au gratin" and other variations. (We never see that nowadays, but revisiting Kommetje a few years ago, the hotel was still advertising "crayfish dinners".) There was a good beach, we could bathe in the sea, and the village people were friendly – paradise! Of course, we had our hours on duty and worked regular watches, though we were not too busy.

Ashore, we could catch one of several Navy transports in the day, to Fish Hoek, where there were trains to Cape Town. Ellison House was the Women's Forces centre in Cape Town, run by the ladies of the SAWAS (South African Women's Auxiliary Service – their equivalent of our WVS), and was very much utilised – and appreciated! – by the Women's Services, South African and British. There was a café, lounges to sit in, and here one could hire a furnished cubicle with a bed for the night for very low prices.

From time to time we would meet, here and elsewhere, members of the newly-formed South African Women's Auxiliary Naval Service

(SWANS), who worked with the South African Naval Force, and were now starting to appear in a uniform similar to ours.

The main disadvantages were the enormous spiders; they must have been as much as 1.5 inches across; and *cobras* – any amount of them. The station was on a headland, and "Slangkop" means "snake's head" in Afrikaans. They were all over the camp; the men would find them in their buckets, etc. and have to deal with them. Occasionally, when walking, we would see one going along the road, near the ditch – they moved astonishingly fast – but fortunately, we never met one on the station.

We would find the spiders sitting on our bedroom light switches when we came off duty at 2 a.m. (The doors opened inwards, and in the dark, one would wonder if a snake would be there!). But there was usually a spider, and one Wren was much in demand, as she was a dab hand at disposing of them!

An English couple, to whom I had been introduced through Guiding soon after arriving, had come out from England. Older than me, they had a flat in Fish Hoek (our railway station, about seven miles from Slangkop) and were extremely kind to me all the time I was there. I was given a key of the flat and told I could drop in whenever I liked – it truly was a "home away from home".

Stella suffered badly from chronic asthma, and was often not at all well. They had a stuffed terrier, made of sheepskin at one of the sewing parties supporting the war effort. He was called "Caesar". I had two stuffed dolls, in Guide and Brownie uniform – "Brenda the Brownie" and "Sybil the Sea Ranger" (originally "Gertie the Guide"), made up of patterns from the *Guide* magazine – and these three could always be found in mischievous positions (such as climbing up the kitchen cupboard shelves) if I had been in while my friends were out. It became quite a competition to see which could outdo the other! We had endless fun together.

Stella had fitted up what was usually a sewing room as my bedroom, and I could come and go as I pleased – coming off duty at 8 a.m., I could catch the morning transport to Fish Hoek, go "home", have a bath and go to bed, and then go shopping or to Cape Town on the train. Sadly, after the war, Stella paid two visits to England, and at the end of the second voyage home to South Africa, she was found dead in her cabin – the asthma had overcome her, and I had lost two very good friends. Fred remarried later, and when I visited Cape Town years afterwards, he came to tea – and a very dusty Caesar emerged from his pocket, to give us all his greetings!

Soon after our arrival, an invitation went up on

the notice board at the Helmsley from the Cape Town Sea Rangers, inviting any Guides or Rangers among us to contact them. Three or four of us, sitting in the fo'c'sle of an evening, decided to respond. I telephoned the given number, and we all received an invitation from Dorothy Greenshields and her husband, Hugh, to spend the evening with them.

Catching the bus to Rondebosch was quite an adventure. The people on the bus all wanted to ask us about the blitz in Britain – one lady thought it quite disgraceful that nobody had asked us out (however, we *were* out but not as she meant!). We found the flat and were joined by some Sea Rangers. After supper, we *insisted* on doing the washing up, rather to their surprise – however, we explained that everyone in England helped to wash up in these days (and often had their supper served in the kitchen too). Afterwards, on my saying to Dorothy that even if I told her where I lived, she would never understand the name of my small Welsh town, to my surprise, Dorothy showed me a postcard of Penmaenmawr, my home – I would never have thought that she would even have heard of that little town, but it turned out that she had come from Manchester! Incidentally, I later found Penmaenmawr mentioned in the *Letters of Lady Anne Barnard*. She was the wife of the first Colonial Secretary of the Cape (this was recommended reading for many people coming to South Africa for the first time).

The Sea Rangers had a rowing boat on a "vlei" – a small lake near the seashore – and any of us off duty used to join them on Saturday afternoons. There were usually a number of us to be found at our "skipper's" hut, "Ship Ashore"; Wrens and Sea Rangers got along well and made good friends, enjoying the sunshine, swimming and rowing.

Later on, many of the sailors at Slangkop (most of whom were survivors from the *Prince of Wales* and the *Repulse*) were drafted back to England from the Cape, as the European War was drawing to a close and the Japanese War had to be planned. However, the latter did not last long. Meantime, the question in everybody's mind was, "When will we be going into Europe?" (Though most of our thoughts at that point in time were with "our boys" in Burma.)

It was winter, a season of torrential rain. One morning, I was sleeping after night duty in my "bedroom", when I was awakened by Stella saying, "Wake up and look outside! There is a river running down the street – and we have gone into Europe!" It was D-day!

Our two and a half years overseas were almost up when VE-day came. Life changed completely. The sailors were "sitting on" the ship-to-shore waves (they would never allow us to do that work!) listening to the German submarines surrendering one by one and receiving instructions regarding the ports to which they should go to give themselves up. We attended the Cape Town victory parade and the celebration in the City Hall.

The Wrens were sent home in triumph on a cruiser, on which, I am told, they worked – and played their part as members of the ship's company. I was also informed that I had been recommended for a commission – too late! Oh, well – I had actually been in the Navy, and that was a privilege, according to Aunt Nancy's teaching!

Unfortunately, I missed most of these events, as I was in hospital with appendicitis, followed by the usual surgery, and did not recover quickly enough. So instead of on the cruiser I had to go home on a hospital ship – the *Tairea* – from Durban to Port Suez (as ships were not taken through the Suez Canal); then a week's stay in a Desert Army hospital; and finally a week in the Royal Naval hospital at Alexandria, before embarking at Port Said for Liverpool on the *Oranje*, a Dutch hospital ship, staffed by the British. (The less said about that journey home, the better!)

Just outside Valetta Harbour, Malta, a friend and I met a bridge lookout, just coming from the upper deck off duty, and looking decidedly ruffled. On being asked what was wrong, he replied that

we would never have a closer call! He told us that
he had been on the bridge and had seen some
soldiers in the bows, pointing at something ahead
– so close to the ship that he could not see it –
"And not one of those landsmen raised the alarm!"
he said. And a few minutes later, a mine floated
past, just a foot or two from the ship's side – a
wicked-looking thing, but it thankfully did not
touch the ship, and we arrived safely at Liverpool
some days later.

After disembarkation leave, sick leave, a time at
Portsmouth Drafting Depot and Burghfield, later
known as *HMS Dauntless*, for remustering (as W/T
was no longer required – and I lost my Leading
rate); then two weeks' refresher course (at which,
surprisingly, I still had my shorthand speeds) at
the Naval Secretarial Training establishment,
Wetherby, Yorkshire (where much time was spent
in cleaning windows with wet newspaper, in the
snow), I was eventually sent to the Flotilla Staff
Office in Admiralty House, Portsmouth Dock-
yard, as writer (special duties) to Commander (D),
Portsmouth. He was in charge of the Portsmouth
Destroyer Flotilla. I had "signed on" again for
another eighteen months, to see if there would be
a permanent WRNS, about which rumours were
circulating – but that service was only announced
just after I had been released and gone home.

At the Portsmouth Flotilla Staff Office, there

were two officers and three writers (one male from the Flotilla and two Wrens) working in a smaller room, opening from the main office. Besides the normal typing, etc., we used to make the tea. We had a small, two-bar electric heater, which we used to put on its back on the floor; on top of this, we would place a large, black "non-electric" enamel kettle to boil – and thus we would make tea for the Flotilla Captains, for their Monday afternoon meetings, as well as for any who might visit the office at any time. Those were the days of improvisation, when many things were in short supply – we used to use Saccharin tablets, but managed to get some milk daily. Tea was rationed, and one Wren was usually employed with a quarter or half-pound package of tea and a pair of tweezers, picking out the "real tea" from the "bush tea"! (We got one or two cups of tea from the package, and had to "enjoy", or the reverse, the "bush" tea for the remainder.)

The work could be punctuated at any time by a shout from next door of "Pickles" – me! – "another cup of tea please!" – and on would go the kettle. None of us ever guessed that we were looking after the captains of the destroyers that had fought the "Battle of the Barents Sea", (or "Murmansk"), when we were working so hard in Greenock, before going overseas.

Quite recently I was given a book on those battles, which included an account of them, and what was my astonishment to read about the first three ships in our Portsmouth Flotilla, to whose captains I had handed many cups of tea. This, then, was the "something big", for which we took down those long reports, perhaps directly from the destroyers *Orwell*, *Obdurate* and *Obedient*, which had been engaged before we left Greenock. I had indeed been meeting with History, both in Greenock and Portsmouth!

Another interesting task was when the Royal Family visited South Africa in 1946; it fell to my lot to type the manoeuvring orders for our destroyers, which were to escort *Vanguard* down the Solent.

I remained in Portsmouth until I was "de-mobbed" in March/April 1947. I was released on the night of "the great freeze-up", when almost everything in Britain froze – including the railways – and I spent my first night as a civilian, on the Portsmouth to London train! I had decided to spend a week of my "demob" leave in London, staying at a service hostel and buying some new civilian clothes with part of my gratuity. This I did, and the following week I caught the express train from Euston to North Wales, arriving home for my demobilisation leave after the best five and a half years of my life!

July 2004, Richmond, BC